The Tree Doctor

THE TREE DOCTOR
A BANTAM BOOK 978 0 857 51363 2

First published in Great Britain by Bantam,
an imprint of Random House Children's Publishers UK
A Random House Group Company

This edition published 2013

Bantam Books are published by Random House Children's Publishers UK,
61–63 Uxbridge Road, London W5 5SA

www.randomhousechildrens.co.uk
www.randomhouse.co.uk

Addresses for companies within The Random House Group Limited can be found at: www.
randomhouse.co.uk/offices.htm

THE RANDOM HOUSE GROUP Limited Reg. No. 954009

A CIP catalogue record for this book is available from the British Library.

Printed in China

The Tree Doctor

By Tish Rabe

From a script by Bernice Vanderlaan

Illustrated by Tom Brannon

BANTAM BOOKS

"Breakfast!" called Sally.

"The pancakes are hot!
Let's find out how much
maple syrup we've got."

"Trees give sap to make syrup,"
said Nick, "but this one
is so small, we can't make
any syrup. No fun!"

"I smell pancakes!" the Cat cried.

"Oh, I hope I am right.

I love golden pancakes,

all fluffy and light,

with sweet maple syrup.

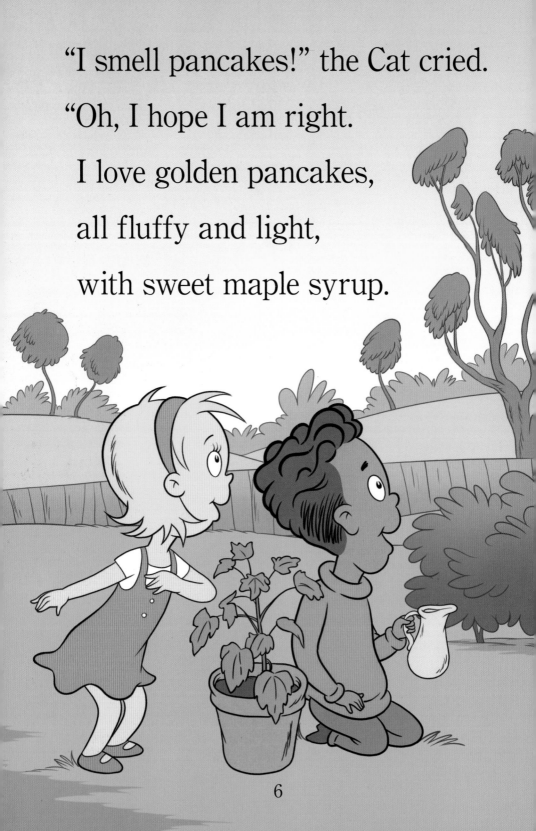

Oh, pour me some, please!

It's my favorite thing

that we get from the trees."

"We've got pancakes," said Nick.

"But unfortunately,

no sap to make syrup

from our maple tree."

"Not to worry!" the Cat said.

"Today I'll take you

to meet the Tree Doctor.

He'll know what to do."

"Meet Dr Twiggles!

He takes care of trees.

He swings through the branches

and hangs by his knees!"

"Hello," said the doctor. "Yes, it's up to me to respond to and treat every tree-mergency!"

Dr Twigberry Twiggles
2 Spruce Street
Wild Woolly Wood

If your pine is in pain or your oak's not OK, call me night or day. I'll be there right away.

"Now, what brings you three
to the Wild Woolly Wood?"
"Our tree's not growing,"
answered Nick, "as it should."

"Little tree," said the doctor,

"how are you feeling?

Are your twigs in a twist?

Has your bark started peeling?"

"Hmm . . . colour's nice and dark.

Stem is not bumpy.

Branches aren't brittle.

Twigs are not lumpy.

But these leaves are drooping,

and that means, I'd say,

I should check your tree's roots

and do so right away."

14

"Check the roots?" Sally asked.

"How can you do that?"

"To the Thinga-ma-jigger!"

cried the Cat in the Hat.

"Flip the Thrilla-ma-driller
and we'll see if it's ill.
If you've never seen tree roots,
well, soon we all will!"

"Look at that," said Nick.

"This really is neat.

The roots of a tree

are like a tree's feet."

"AbsoROOTly!" the Cat cried.
"I happen to know
roots soak up food and water
and help a tree grow."

"I've got it!" the doc said.

"Now I see why

your tree isn't growing.

The soil is too dry."

"It needs water?" the Cat asked.

"I know what to do.

This is a job

for Thing One and Thing Two!"

Those two Things jumped out,
and they gave a big yank
to the crank on the side
of the Thinga-ma-tank.

But they turned it too far
and they turned it too fast.
Water shot out in a
soaking-wet blast!

"Good job!" said the doc.
"But our work is not done.
To get healthy, your tree
needs to get lots of sun."
"I know!" cried the Cat.
"Your tree will feel right
when my Brighta-ma-lighter
gives it sunlight."

"Now just wait," said the doc.
"In forty years you can tap
your tree and make syrup
from the maple tree sap."

"Forty years!" said Nick.
"When our tree is that old,
our stack of pancakes
will REALLY be cold!"

"No problem!" said the doc.
"For I have right here
some syrup I made
in the spring of last year.

And I have something else -
a bag of maple keys,
full of maple tree seeds
to grow even more trees."

Back home, Nick said,
"This syrup is good
and I had lots of fun
in the Wild Woolly Wood."
"Eat up!" said the Cat.
"Then I need your help, please.
After breakfast let's go
and plant . . .

". . . more maple trees!"